Disney · PIXAR
THE INCREDIBLES

LEVEL 4

Re-told by: Helen Parker
Series Editor: Melanie Williams

Pearson Education Limited
Edinburgh Gate, Harlow,
Essex CM20 2JE, England
and Associated Companies throughout the world.

ISBN: 978-1-4082-8868-9

This edition first published by Pearson Education Ltd 2013

3 5 7 9 10 8 6 4 2

Set in 17/21pt OT Fiendstar
Printed in China
SWTC/02

Published by Pearson Education Ltd in association with
Penguin Books Ltd, both companies being subsidiaries of Pearson Plc.

For a complete list of the titles available in the Penguin Kids series please go to www.penguinreaders.com.
Alternatively, write to your local Pearson Education office or to: Penguin Readers Marketing Department,
Pearson Education, Edinburgh Gate, Harlow, Essex CM20 2JE, England.

Mr. Incredible was very strong and very smart. He was the world's best superhero!

Buddy was Mr. Incredible's biggest fan. He was a normal boy, but he wanted to work with Mr. Incredible. Buddy invented rocket boots. Now he could fly!

"Fly home!" said Mr. Incredible. He did not want any help from Buddy.

3

Elastigirl was Mr. Incredible's wife. She was a superhero who could change the shape of her body. She loved Mr. Incredible and their life was very exciting.

But then their life changed. People did not want help from the superheroes anymore. They wanted the superheroes to hide their powers. They wanted them to be normal people.

Mr. Incredible became Bob Parr and Elastigirl became Helen Parr. Soon, they had three children. Violet, their daughter, could become invisible and make force fields. Dash, their son, could run super fast. The baby, Jack-Jack, was normal — or that was what the family thought.

Dinnertime in the Parr house was often very interesting!

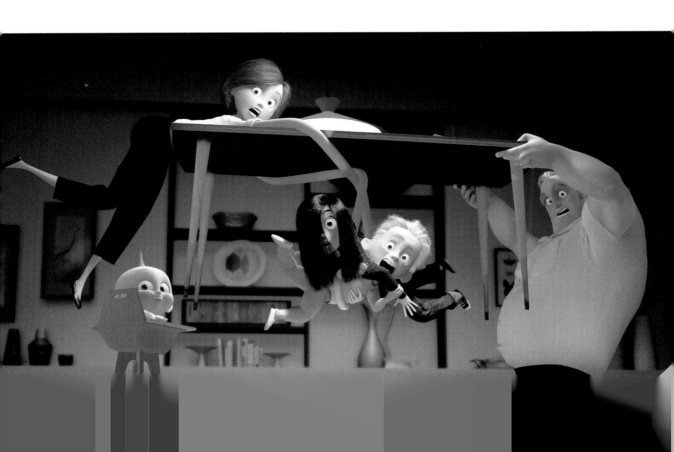

Bob got a normal job. It was very boring.

One day at work, Bob saw a thief in the street. The thief hit a man. Bob wanted to help the man, but his boss stopped him. Bob pushed his boss softly.

CRASH!

His boss went through five walls ... and Bob lost his job!

Bob went home. He opened his bag. A computer fell out and a woman started to speak. "My name is Mirage," she said. "I have an important job for you, Mr. Incredible ... You must stop the Omnidroid. It's a very dangerous robot. My boss can pay you a lot of money."

Bob was excited. He wanted this new job.

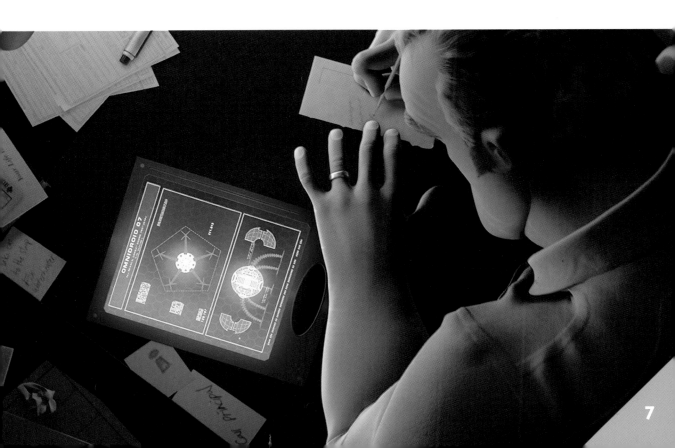

Bob flew to the island of Nomanisan and met with Mirage inside a volcano. He did not tell Helen or his children about his new work.

"Stop the Omnidroid," said Mirage. "Do it quickly ... and don't die!"

Mr. Incredible soon found the Omnidroid. It was smart, but Mr. Incredible was smarter. He fought the robot and won!

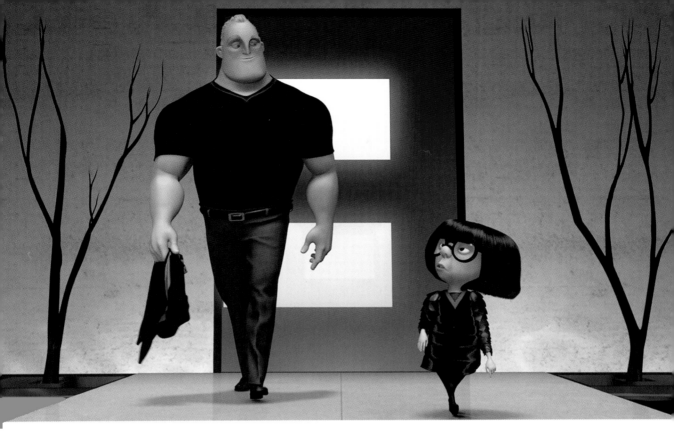

Bob was very happy with his new work. He went to Edna Mode's house. Edna made suits for superheroes. She made Bob a new suit. He loved it! (She also made new suits for his family but she did not tell Bob.)

Mirage had a new job for Mr. Incredible. He flew to Nomanisan in his new suit.

Suddenly, a new Omnidroid attacked Mr. Incredible. It was stronger and smarter than the last one. Mr. Incredible lost the fight.

A man in a black suit and rocket boots arrived. "Now my invention is ready! It can beat Mr. Incredible," he said. "And I *am* your biggest fan!"

"Buddy?" said Mr. Incredible.

"My name's Syndrome now!" the man shouted.

Mr. Incredible escaped from Syndrome. He went into the volcano and opened Syndrome's computer. Syndrome wanted to send the Omnidroid into the city. Then Syndrome could beat it and pretend to be a superhero.

Back at home, Helen wanted to know where Bob was. She went to Edna Mode's house. She was surprised to see her family's new suits!

The suits had computers in them. Helen used the computer in her suit. It found Bob.

A loud noise came from Bob's suit. **BEEP!** Syndrome was now inside the volcano. He heard the noise and put Bob in a force field.

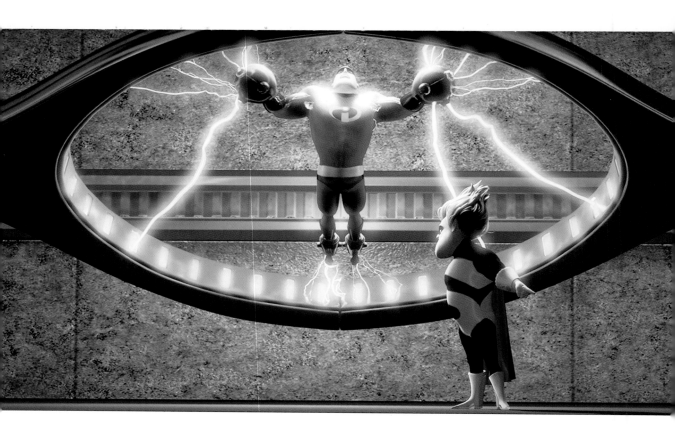

Helen took a plane and flew to Nomanisan. Violet and Dash left Jack-Jack with a friend and followed her.

Helen found her children on the plane and was angry …
But then Syndrome attacked!

BOOM! They fell into the ocean. Helen became a boat
and Dash pushed the boat super fast!

Soon they arrived on the island. Helen wanted to find Bob.

"Be strong," she told the children. "Here you can use your
powers." Dash and Violet were excited that they were able
to use their powers.

Helen fought Syndrome's men and found her husband inside the volcano. Bob was very happy to see her!

In the jungle, Syndrome's men saw Dash and Violet. They wanted to catch the children. Dash ran away super fast and Violet became invisible.

Helen and Bob found the children in time. The family used their super powers and fought the men.

But then Syndrome arrived. He caught the family in a force field. They could not move!

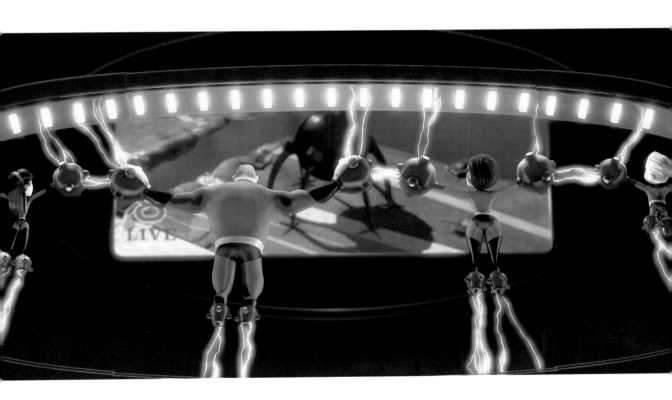

Syndrome talked about his big plan. On TV, they could see the new Omnidroid. It was now in the city!

"I'm going to be a bigger superhero than you, Mr. Incredible!" said Syndrome. Then he got into a plane and flew to the city.

Mr. Incredible felt terrible. His family was in this dangerous place because he wanted to be a superhero again.

Very quietly, Violet made a new force field and escaped. She saved her family!

Quickly, the family – the Incredibles! – ran from Syndrome's force field. They found a rocket and flew to the city. They had to stop Syndrome!

In the city, the Omnidroid attacked. The people were really scared.

Suddenly, Syndrome flew above the Omnidroid. He used a remote control and pretended to hit the robot. One of the Omnidroid's arms fell to the ground.

But the Omnidroid was very smart. It hit Syndrome and the remote control flew out of his hand.

The Incredibles arrived in the city and the Omnidroid attacked them.

The family used their super powers and fought the robot. But the Omnidroid was very strong. It threw Mr. Incredible through a building. SMASH!

Mr. Incredible was okay. He got up and saw Syndrome's remote control on the ground ...

Mr. Incredible threw the remote control away from the robot. Dash ran super fast and caught it.

Then Mr. Incredible found the Omnidroid's arm. Elastigirl used the remote control and the arm flew through the air and hit the Omnidroid.

CRASH! The Omnidroid fell to the ground and died.

The Incredibles saved the city and the people loved them again!

At last the family could go home. They went into their house, but Syndrome was there! And Jack-Jack was in his arms!

"You took my future!" said Syndrome. "Now I am taking yours!"

He flew out of the house with the baby.

In the air, Jack-Jack suddenly changed. He became a ball of fire and attacked Syndrome.

Syndrome quickly dropped Jack-Jack and flew to his plane.

Bob threw Helen into the air and she caught Jack-Jack.
Then he threw a car at Syndrome's plane.

BOOM! The plane fell to the ground and Syndrome died.
Violet made a force field and saved her family from the
falling plane.

"That's my girl!" said Helen.

The Incredibles have a normal life again, but they are much happier now.

They usually hide their super powers, but sometimes they have to use them ...

Sometimes they have to put on their red and black suits and save the world! Thank you, Incredibles!

Before You Read

1 Find a page with ...
1 a robot
2 a superhero
3 a volcano
4 a force field
5 a remote control

2 Look at this picture. Talk or write about this family.

After You Read

① **Match the name to the super power.**

1	Mr. Incredible	**a** can run super fast.
2	Elastigirl	**b** can become a ball of fire.
3	Violet	**c** can change shape.
4	Dash	**d** can make force fields and become invisible.
5	Jack-Jack	**e** is super strong and super smart.

② **Answer the questions.**

1 What did Buddy invent? Why?

2 Why did Bob push his Boss?

3 What was the Omnidroid?

4 What was Syndrome's plan?

5 How did the Incredibles stop the Omnidroid?

6 Why did Syndrome drop Jack-Jack?

③ **Who said it? Match the sentence to the person.**

1 "Stop the Omnidroid. Do it quickly ... and don't die!"

2 "Here you can use your powers."

3 "Fly home!"

4 "And I *am* your biggest fan!"

Mr. Incredible
Syndrome
Mirage
Helen

④ **Write the names of some famous superheroes. Which is your favorite? Why?**